# A

# KILLER

# CALLED

# COMFORT

*Danger is Lurking in America's Churches*

## BY PAT SPELL BLACKWELL

# DEDICATION

To Elwood

Who looked beyond my flaws

and saw my potential.

This one's for you.

Happy Birthday!!

# CONTENTS

# ACKNOWLEDGMENTS

I have always enjoyed reading the acknowledgments in other books but often wondered why there were so many. Well, now I know! Myriads of people have offered help, support, and encouragement in significant ways. I have tried to keep a running list and pray I've not left anyone out. Each of you filled a place that needed filling. For that, I am truly grateful.

Thank you, Charlana Kelly, The Book Doula! Friend, confidante, sister, and expert. I remain humbled by your love and encouragement even when I was screaming and you were saying, *"Push! Push!"* You are my forever friend, and I love you. You invited me to connect, inspired me to grow, and prodded me to more—all for the glory of God.

Courtenay Blackwell Collins, my writing buddy, and artistic role model. Thank you for your willingness to brainstorm the topic of the day. You're a gifted creator (among other things). I love you.

Scott Miker, author of *You Can't Surf from the Shore*, graciously entrusted his words to me.

Thank you to my steadfast reading friends who took the time to make enthusiastic recommendations: Sarah Spoerl, Derald Gall, Shelia Witt Michele, Heidi Darst, Lourdes Relyea, Shirley Page, Don Estes, Teri Counselman, Nancy Harding Burgess, Debi Kittles, Beth Corbett Houser, John Leard, Reggie Pennington, and Daniel Painter.

Thank you, Lori Blackwell, who is my sister from the family of God but not from the family of Blackwell. You are my research assistant extraordinaire, exuberant encourager, and faithful friend.

And especially, Courtenay Collins, Crosby Kirkowski, Cody Tobin, Sarah Murano-Gordon, and Xochilth Hernandez, my precious daughters who often put up with me, sometimes tolerate me, and always love me! Your support for this project has been invaluable. Your willingness to always believe and encourage the best of me is a treasure. Your faith, hope, and love inspire me. Your daddy and I are so proud of you. I love each of you with my whole heart and my big toe!

# FOREWORD

"A Killer Named Comfort" is a timely message from a woman with a passion for Jesus, the Gospel, and people. By this, Pat Spell Blackwell obviously wants the world to know Jesus and receive salvation through faith in Him.

I have known her personally for decades and watched her help, teach, counsel, and disciple people during those years. Through it all, her love shines as she sets an example for Christians, demonstrating what it looks like to take in a stranger, feed the hungry, and give drink to the thirsty. Whether spiritual or natural substance, she rarely denied someone in need. I've also witnessed her raw admissions in the Preface/Introduction of her book. While she may think otherwise, it's been an absolute joy to watch God move on her in such marvelous ways. Something I'm sure others have marveled at too.

In her riveting book "A Killer Called Comfort," she manages to express the depths of her heart for the church and believers worldwide. A wake-up call to the masses, Pat reminds us of how easy it is for believers to fall away from their first love, compromise, become lukewarm, corrupt, and ultimately experience spiritual death. Say it isn't so!

Ah, but alas, it is accurate, and the Scriptures foretell us so that we can fore-arm ourselves with truth and determination not just to finish our race but help others finish theirs as we fulfill The Great Commission.

There is a danger; it is comfort masquerading in our churches, lulling God's people asleep so that we miss the cues, the warnings, and the blaring sirens going off all around us. Father, give us eyes to see, ears to hear, and hearts that respond with what is right and true in Your eyes.

Pat is not just passionate, she's driven to be a voice in this hour, an encourager, and supporter of people God brings her way. She reminds me of a little girl who found a baby bird fallen out of the nest. She would do anything to get that one back to safety and security nestled beneath the feathers of the Almighty. I hear her pleas in this book, and I'm sure you will too.

She masterfully gives her readers a peak into what it looks like to be under the influence of comfort. She details what went wrong, giving action steps for unsuspecting believers who find themselves among the descriptive stories she uses to paint pictures of the once faithful, now fallen Christ-follower.

Her message is a must-read for every believer. My prayer for you is to take a hard look at your heart and allow the Holy Spirit to reveal the reality of areas that need to awaken and be restored in faith and truth. Ask God to search you and know you, see if there is any way in you that needs cleansing and restoration so that you can serve Him fully and do your part, like Pat, to lead others to Christ.

Thank you, Pat, for letting the Holy Spirit break your heart through an encounter with God's heart. Thank you for giving yourself entirely to exploring this topic and writing this book. Thank you for loving people and God's truth with such zeal that no one can get past you without a simple question. And, I quote, "Do you remember a time when you gave your heart to Jesus?" Depending on the answer, that person will either rejoice that they know Christ too or be brought to a face-to-face encounter with their Savior and Lord.

May we all walk with fervency for Christ refusing to allow a killer called comfort to lull us to sleep anymore!

I love you dearly!

Charlana Kelly, Author TV/Radio Host
Founder, Women of Influence Network
CEO, SpeakTruth Media Group LLC

# PREFACE

I remember when I had prophecies spoken over me and went out in the spirit, sensing the Holy Ghost tingles. I remember hearing prophecies spoken over others and wondering how those things might come to pass in the world. I didn't even consider the things spoken over me, nor do I even remember them. I realized that I had an assumption of doubt! The things seemed too big, too distant, too impossible from my small-minded and limited human brain. I was so immature in my faith and the knowledge of the Word of God, indeed ignorant in my understanding of God Himself, that I never even considered that those things might be possible. I just ignored them. And I ignored Him as well.

I have wondered if God ignored me too. In my foolishness, thinking I did not need Him, did He just leave me alone in my doubt? I know better than that! I know that He has been with me daily, revealing Himself to me through many years and circumstances. He has been ever faithful to me. Romans 2:4 reminds us, "...That the goodness of God leads you to repentance." He watched over and protected me until I finally recognized His immense goodness and came to Him. I have grown in faith and wisdom and longing to do whatever He has for me to do, and while I have not (nor will I ever) "arrive," I am a seeker as never before. I am hungry for His will in my life! I'm thirsty for the knowledge of God! I'm craving more of Him and yielding more of me to Him. It is both a glorious place and a daunting place. I expect Him to show up for me, and the Word says that I will indeed be filled like never before. The daunting part is that I desperately want to stay yielded to His will and His purpose and not let my ideas or projects and behaviors get in the way of what He might have for me!

Perhaps you, too, have been in a place of ignoring God. People who ignore God are everywhere. Some are lost and immersed in the world. And some are sitting in the church pew next to you! There are many reasons for that separation. I believe one of the main reasons is the lack of teaching and revelation. Many today are not in church or attend a church that does not present the Word of God accurately or, disappointingly, offers it without fire or unction or anointing of the Holy Spirit. Maybe you, like myself at times in my life, were rebellious, believing that you could handle your life and your situations yourself and had no need of God's love, direction, or provision. How silly we must seem to our Heavenly Father! But just as a mother loves her child who has grandiose ideas, likewise He is patient with us and still pours out His love on us.

But the days are gone when we can be little children with big self-proclaimed ideas, or worse, immature and rebellious teens who don't think they need God! It is time to assess our hearts and motives and step into a place where we can fully acknowledge Him and His goodness and become the mature, love-filled believer who honors God.

This book will look at what I call comfortable Christianity as I share what the Holy Spirit put on my heart regarding spiritual conditions that need improvement. Changes that will protect the believer from error and deception while spurring them to action as they add to the kingdom of God.

We will also explore insights about growing as a believer and strategies to receive more revelation from Jesus. We all want that. Right? We all need that.

Introduction

# GOD BROKE MY HEART

This book was born from a place of disdain, impatience, even anger. I looked around and self-righteously judged people that I saw doing little, in MY definition, to promote the kingdom of God. In my arrogance, I complained especially about those I saw in the church who were not meeting my expectations of what serving God should look like in the life of a believer. My words were not always kind and were even mocking as I called them Casserole Christians and derided them as people who loved others, mostly their own Sunday school classes. I joked that they would even bake you a casserole! I was mean-spirited and I didn't even realize it at first.

Then the Holy Spirit caught me up short when He reminded me that these Casserole Christians were part of His church. That they were His bride, and that He loved them and, guess what? That I should love them too! It was a humbling time, and I felt great shame. If not for my understanding of His forgiveness and mercy, I would still be ashamed and certainly not willing to admit how truly ugly my heart was at that time.

In retrospect, I saw that my ideas of how Christians were lacking were really truths that needed to be addressed. My approach and thoughts were far from anything God would approve of or allow me to say! So, I threw the notes I had made about the issues in a drawer and began to pray for forgiveness. And for my heart to change, and my words, and my attitude. God showed up as He always does when we ask. And He broke my heart.

I began to try and define what my heart for my readers was. It was not an easy process. I had to toss out a lot of negative thinking and pursue what God might be thinking about them. The issues were real, but my attitude had to reflect the love and care of Father God for people who were missing the mark in a complicated world. It was a work of change bathed in tears.

"Humility is not an innate trait; it must be learned. Many mistake humility for weakness. But humility is a great heart opener. It's hard to refuse anything to a humble heart." This quote by Bangambiki Habyarimana in his "Book of Wisdom," touched my heart and challenged me to address people differently. So I began to explore what was happening with the folks I was thinking about but in kinder, gentler ways. The result was a new term to me: Comfortable Christianity. My heart was changed, even renewed, toward comfortable Christians. Let me share with you how my concerns for them developed.

First, I became worried that since many believers function from a place of comfort, as end times become more challenging, those folks might experience a crisis of faith and turn away from the Lord. In the Scripture it is a falling away that has been called the Great Apostasy. It is a falling away of believers, not those in the world! I believe we are living out Matthew 24 and that our circumstances will worsen as the time of Jesus' return approaches. From Matthew 24:6-8, we shall hear of wars and rumors of wars and nation will rise up against nation and kingdom against kingdom. There will be famines, pestilences (diseases), and earthquakes in various places— the beginning of sorrows, as it were. And Jesus said that these things must come to pass. But the trouble for believers continues in verses 9—12, where we read that the enemy will deliver you up to tribulation (not yet the Great Tribulation) and kill you, and all nations will hate you for Jesus' name's sake. And at that point, many believers will be offended and betray one another and hate one another. Then many false prophets will rise up and deceive many, and because lawlessness will abound, the love of many will grow cold. These verses were written about believers who will be caught off guard, deceived, chastened by outside forces, betray fellow Christians, become lawless, and their love of God will grow cold, even nonexistent. In his footnotes in The Spirit-filled Life Bible, Jack Hayford states succinctly: "There will be religious deception, social and political upheavals, natural calamities, disloyalty, and persecution--all of which are precursors of the end times."

My concern also extended to the fact that because comfortable Christians will grow cold towards the things of God, they will surely miss opportunities to see Jesus revealed in a dying world that continues to need Him desperately. In their Christian walk, these comfortable Christians are now unfulfilled, even bored, and worse, might not even know it! We need holy boldness, not unholy bored-ness!

Following that thought, I realized that comfortable Christians have so much to offer others but do not know how to offer it to those in need. I pray that each one will recognize the gifts and talents God has lovingly and uniquely placed in them. They are an untapped resource for the kingdom of God! We as believers have everything we need to share our God with others because *"His divine power has given to us all things that pertain to life and godliness, through the knowledge of Him who called us by glory and virtue"* (2 Peter 1:3). God Himself, through the Holy Spirit, has equipped us for every task!

And lastly, I hoped that each of these comfortable Christians would be stirred and challenged to grow and affect the kingdom of God. That they would be motivated to win souls, help people get out of their misery and live a life embraced by God Himself, and function daily in righteousness, peace, and joy in the Holy Ghost. We cannot ignore the challenge Jesus left us in Mark 16:15—18: *"Go and Preach! Cast out demons! Lay hands on the sick! Get people out of their misery and into the kingdom of righteousness, peace, and joy in the Holy ghost! The kingdom of God"* (TPT).

Revival is what this is all about. Seeing the lackluster places and recognizing that something must change asking the Holy Spirit to "fire us up" and set us on a path to affect that change! Then, preparing ourselves by honing those skills and gifts God has ordained for us to live out with the help and direction of the Holy Spirit, and getting out of our la-Z-Boys and into a world that is longing for a way of redemption, healing, and true freedom! O Lord, renew in us the joy of our salvation!

Chapter One

# A WORD ABOUT COMFORTABLE BELIEVERS

So why are we even having a conversation about comfortable Christianity? Why is it necessary to define it, point it out, or do something about it? Because the earmark of comfort becomes the stain of complacency. Complacency is born of deception. Deception leads to destruction. In the following pages, I am going to tell you some stories that represent those folks that God broke my heart over. Accounts where you might recognize someone you've heard of, someone you know, or even yourself. Bear with me while I set it up, then let's visit some people!

In Matthew 24, Jesus is talking with the disciples as He often did. He had predicted the destruction of the temple, and His disciples had questions. They came to him privately on the Mount of Olives wanting to know what to expect regarding the signs of the times and the end of the age. *"Tell us, when will these things be? And what will be the sign of Your coming and the end of the age?"* (Matthew 24:3). Jesus was very clear with His answer to them in verse 4: *"Take heed that no one deceives you."* He then went on to describe what those last days would look like in the following ten verses. It is not a pretty picture. We'll look at those things a bit later.

Deception is the most significant sign of the return of Christ and we're living in a time of deception that has never been experienced before. Deception is not often a big boogeyman that jumps out from behind a tree on a dark road. Like the devil himself, deception is subtle and cunning and reassuring and provides a false sense of well-being that says, oh, that little thing, it's no big deal. Unfortunately, deception has crept up on believers in ways that seem innocuous and non-threatening. Deception has made evil appear good and good seem evil and has tricked many Christians into believing that it is okay to be just a little bit off from what we know as truth in the name of acceptance and love. Diversity and inclusion, and political correctness, have drawn many believers to a misguided place of watered-down truth of the Word of God and set them up for being ineffective in their walk with God.

> *"Diversity and inclusion, and political correctness, have drawn many believers to a misguided place of watered-down truth of the Word of God..."*

Scripture admonishes us to avoid being deceived. James tells us in Chapter 1 verse 22: *"But be doers of the word and not hearers only,* deceiving yourselves." *Have you ever really considered that you may be deceiving yourself? Jack Hayford's commentary regarding this verse in the Spirit-filled Life Bible is succinct: "Salvation leads to service. It is self-deception to believe that God's goal for church attendance is merely to hear the word, instead to experience a transformation of life that results in ministry."* He continues, *"Obedience to the Word of God brings about the work of God. We are to hear the word and do the work. To hear and do nothing is one sign of a deceived heart. Faith acts. To believe is to do"* (Emphasis mine)!

From this, he challenges believers to evaluate the areas of our lives where we claim to have faith, yet our actions declare unbelief. We must practice what we proclaim!

James Chapter 2 further instructs us that we are to show our faith alive by acting upon it. And while we know that works will not save us (only Jesus' atonement on the cross can do that), our faith without works is considered dead.

James 2:14-19: *"What does it profit, my*

*brethren, if someone says he has faith but does not have works? Can faith save him? If a brother or sister is naked and destitute of daily food, and one of you says to them, "be warmed and filled,"* but you do not give them the things which are needed for the body, what does it profit? Thus, also faith by itself, if it does not have works, is dead. But someone will say, 'You have faith, and I have works.' Show me your faith without works, and I will show you my faith by my works. You believe that there is one God. You do well. Even the demons believe—and tremble!"

Mark Twain is credited with the following statement: *"It is easier to fool the people than convince the people that they have been fooled."* As we look at comfortable Christianity, I urge you to keep this statement in mind. It is easy to think that the points made here apply to others and not to ourselves. But let's look honestly at some soft factors of church comfort.

There are many people happily inside church walls, singing praises, loving on friends, family, and fellow believers, who have lulled themselves with self-satisfaction, never growing, never reaching out as they allow a desperate and fallen world to pass them by every day. No, let me rephrase that, allowing individuals, your neighbor, the grocery store clerk, your mechanic, yardman, doctor's receptionist, cousin, whomever, to face life's difficulties without knowing the only real solution to their faults, their fears, or their dilemmas: that Jesus has a plan for their lives because He loves them sacrificially. And too many believers are perfectly content to let that be so. They are comfortable.

Comfortable is a great word. One definition from the Merriam-Webster Dictionary says, *"enjoying a place of contentment and security."* Another says, *"as large as is needed or wanted."* The latter makes me think of wide country porches and colorful cozy quilts. But there is more. Broadly, the definition continues, "anything that encourages serenity or well-being or complacency." We'll come back to that word complacency in a bit. Another explanation was *"a sense of physical or psychological ease, often characterized as a lack of hardship.*" Then I got hung up on comfortable synonyms and those definitions. Easy can mean *"without anything that caused discomfort or constraints,"* while snug was described as "just enough space for comfort and safety but no more." I had to think about that one. It brought me back to the old *"us four, no more"* attitude that has been observed in some churches through the years. Simply put, what we have is enough. We are satisfied (even happy) with where we are, and there is no need to get more. Comfortable, cozy, snug, and easy.

Now let's look at the definition for complacency: *"a feeling of quiet pleasure or security, often while unaware of some potential danger or defect; or self-satisfaction with the existing condition or situation."* Scott Miker, author of You Can't Surf from the Shore, defines being complacent as "pleased, especially with oneself or one's merits, advantages, or situation, often without awareness of some potential danger or defect." Simply put, being happy with oneself and unconcerned for others. He describes complacency in a relationship as feeling so satisfied and secure that you think you don't need to try any harder. It's okay to set the cruise control! The problem is that complacent people never work to reach their potential individually or in relationships because they feel they can quickly deal with any situations that arise. That feeling of calm satisfaction with our own abilities prevents us from trying harder. Unfortunately, we also fail to recognize or disregard actual dangers or deficiencies!

Many believers today seem content to keep doing what they have been doing for many years: church attendance, fellowship, caring for their social group with visits or casseroles. They serve at church as well: choir, teaching Sunday school, planning committees for church administration, and the like. While functioning in your social circle is comfortable and fun, it may not bring the challenges that will help you develop the call that Jesus placed on your life when you were born again. I submit that those acting out these roles have been deceived, believing that they honor

Jesus and serve Him. But because their hearts are far from Him, their perfunctory activities are only righteous in their own eyes and are merely filthy rags to Him!

Some have said there is no such thing as *"retirement"* in the Bible, yet there are many (of all ages) who have retired from the Lord's work— retired from obedience to the Great Commission. Let's consider "seasoned" believers who are often susceptible to comfort and complacency. Perhaps they are dealing with aging and aches and pains, waning energies, and fewer life responsibilities. Many have survived a lifetime of challenges and now have less drama, a more even emotional keel, a leveling out, if you will, where high places are low and crooked places are straight. Many are living in an easy, comfortable place. Yet this is not an invitation to coast! Many Christians are deceived, believing that they have already "done their part" and have a smug satisfaction that it is no longer their responsibility to work for the kingdom of God. They are unaware of the dangers that are lurking outside their small and self-centered world. That, my friends, is complacency. Complacency is not only detrimental to the believer's relationship with the Father but also dangerous! When testing comes their way, they may find that the strength and foundation of faith needed to face hard times may be waning and weak. And that makes them an easy target for the enemy satan. I've called it comfortable Christianity, but it is more than that. All too often, it is complacent Christianity, which is a significant problem for the kingdom of God. And it's a significant problem for individuals living in that kingdom a well.

> *"Many Christians are deceived, believing that they have already "done their part" and have a smug satisfaction that it is no longer their responsibility to work for the kingdom of God."*

First Peter 5:8 admonishes us: "Be sober, be vigilant; because your adversary the devil walks about like a roaring lion, seeking whom he may devour." No one wants to be a lion's Snackable!

Verse 9 continues, "Resist him, steadfast in the faith..." Just as a lion in the wild goes after his prey, we must likewise be diligent to avoid the attack of the devil. Lions seek out the smallest animal, one who is injured, or the animal who has drifted away from the protection of the herd. As we face an enemy that wants to destroy us, we must remember that he too goes after the one who is weak, wounded, or wandering! We must stand against the devil attempting to destroy our lives, and we cannot do that from a position of comfort nor complacency!

As we look at comfort or even complacency, our goal is not to judge, condemn or convict. Instead, the purpose of this book is to enlighten, teach, encourage, prepare, strengthen, and free believers to enter a place of connection and companionship with our God, Jesus, and the Holy Spirit. Only in that place of relationship can we truly live in righteousness, peace, and joy!

In the following chapters we will meet some believers who are comfortable. While some of them may seem familiar, these are fictional characters who represent traits and behaviors demonstrating what can go wrong in our Christian walk and lead us into deception.

Chapter Two

# A WORD ABOUT
# LOVELESS CHRISTIANS

Angie and David fell in love in their early twenties. David was working in an insurance job which he loved and was experiencing great success in it. Promotions and bonuses came regularly, and he was on the fast track to having his own office and team. Angie was starting her last year of college, finishing her degree in elementary education. Excited about the prospect of having her own classroom, she was already gathering special items to incorporate her style and personality into her teaching. The sun was bright on each of them, and life was good, but it was about to get better.

Introduced by a mutual friend at a community Fourth of July event, Angie and David were immediately drawn to one another. Each carried a zeal for life, and their positive outlooks and anticipation for the future reflected shared values. They dated for the remainder of the summer, became engaged at Thanksgiving, and in late spring, they were married in the church they had begun attending together.

Their early marriage looked like most early marriages. Their main goal was to be together, and they cherished both quality *and* quantity time. Conversations were long, and each of them treasured both listening and sharing and hung on to each other's words. They expressed their hopes and dreams and delighted in the possibilities that lay ahead. David and Angie were eager to serve each other. David loved to try and surprise Angie with thoughtful gifts or a phone call at unexpected times during the day just to say he was thinking of her. Angie did the same for her husband, and he would often find a note telling him how much she loved him. Anxious to please the other, their own desires became secondary, and no sacrifice was too much to serve or honor each other. It was a glorious golden time.

Twenty-seven years and four kids later, life is different: not so golden anymore. They live a peaceable life and are happy enough. They still spend time together but usually with friends or family or at business functions. Neither Angie nor David can remember the last time they had a *"date"* with just the two of them. Now their conversations usually center on the kids, what is happening with them. They talk about the busy schedule each has with work obligations, church commitments, or community service activities. Their days are filled, just not with each other. They have forgotten their first love. And they are comfortable.

## WHAT WENT WRONG?

So how did Angie and David get to this point?

An ignored glance, a forgotten anniversary? Perhaps. It was likely not some significant disturbance but a drip, drip, drip of inattentiveness that simply wore away what was once important. Maybe it was love offered but unreciprocated. A little rejection here and a little rejection there until it was easier just to ignore what was happening than to address it, or maybe those minor slights were not even noticed at all. Sad. Very sad. It was worse. Destructive.

> *"Becoming inattentive is precisely how we slip out of our relationship with God and into a comfortable routine that has little or nothing to do with Him."*

Becoming inattentive is precisely how we slip out of our relationship with God and into a comfortable routine that has little or nothing to do with Him.

You must know this, however. Our God desires a relationship with us! Therefore, He will never fail to respond when we approach Him, or call His name, or offer ourselves to Him in affection. He will never ignore you. He will never forget you, and He will never let you down.

I clearly remember the day I gave my heart to Jesus. I was seven. My mama had dropped me off at Wyomina Park Baptist Church which was not too far from our house. I think my Aunt Betty and Uncle Harold attended that church, but they weren't there that day because I distinctly remember sitting by myself. I don't remember a single word the pastor said during the sermon, nor the songs we sang, but when he started talking about allowing Jesus to come into your heart, I was awestruck. My heart was pounding, and I knew that I *had* to ask Jesus to come into my heart and my life! The pastor took a while to get to the *"invitation,"* and by the time he asked those who wanted Jesus to come to the front, I was already out of my seat in the pew and heading toward the altar! I didn't run, I don't think, at least not in my body, but my spirit was racing to Jesus! Those few seconds are indelibly etched in my memory. It was glorious!

Now in the Baptist church, when someone goes forward to make a decision to follow Jesus, the congregation will *"extend the hand of Christian fellowship."* That means that when the service is done, everyone, and I mean *everyone*, files by and shakes your hand or hugs you to welcome you into the family of God. It takes a while. Thinking back, I was probably a bit (or maybe a lot!) of an oddity being only seven and alone and obviously intent on finding Jesus. So, after many hands and many hugs, I went outside to find my mama.

Again, the picture is so vivid in my mind. My parents had a new 1957 Chevy, turquoise with sleek rear fins. It was a two-door hardtop with windows that rolled all the way down so that the car was wide open. Very cool! The parking lot was nearly empty, and mama was sitting sideways in the driver's seat, feet on the ground. She was wearing red short-shorts and a white off-shoulder halter top with eyelet lace around the neckline, smoking a cigarette. I have no idea why that image has stuck in my mind, but that and the words she spoke to me that morning have echoed in my mind for decades. *"What? Did you go and join the church or something?"* she said as she stamped out her cigarette and turned to drive us home. That was it, no questions, no discussion about why I was late, no follow-up or support of any kind regarding my decision. I was on my own with Jesus. And you know what? I was okay with that. I had fallen in love with Jesus that morning. And I knew He loved me too.

Do you remember when you first asked Jesus into your heart? Is your story clear? Do you have a defining moment? I often ask people I meet this question as a way to learn whether the person I'm talking with is a believer. The answer is often a clear yes, and I have the privilege of hearing their salvation story. Other times their answer is *no* or a wishy-washy, *I think so,* that provides me an opportunity to tell them about Jesus and the impact He has in my life. Then I get to lead them in a prayer of recommitment or salvation.

I believe it is important to remember when you first met Jesus. We remember when we met our spouse, or our best friend, or a favorite neighbor. I have a story about that as well involving my very large glass of iced tea and my neighbor's very small white dog (Sorry, Marge!), but alas, that must wait for another day! The relationships that matter to us are what we think about most. Angie and David remember when they first met. They remember conversations and moments that bound their hearts together. Well, at least they *did.* Until their love grew cold, and they forgot.

There are many believers whose love for Jesus has grown cold. In those early days with Him, praying was easy because we had so much to tell Him. And listening was easy as well because we saw His hand everywhere we looked. He revealed Himself to us, and the time we spent in prayer or praise or studying the Bible was a treasure to us. We just wanted to be with Him. We cherished that connection just as Angie and David did in those early days of marriage.

So how does love grow cold? I am not an expert on this, and probably neither are you, but we can all come up with some causative factors in waning love. Let's take a minute and try and fill in the blanks. I'll list a few things but add your own ideas as we go.

First, time passes—lots of time. Historically,

Jewish tradition and culture allowed one whole year for newlyweds to focus on each other. Therefore, fewer responsibilities and demands were made on the couple. That makes for a rich honeymoon year! *Love is blind* usually refers to one covering the flaws in the person that is loved, but I think it is just as valid to say that love *"blindness"* extends to the world around the lovers and that they indeed only have eyes for each other! As time goes on and the initial delight in new love settles a bit, it is easy to get more comfortable in that love. The once-consuming focus shifts as we become distracted or take on busyness that separates us from our first love: work, bills, kids, neighbors, job opportunities, hobbies, pets, travels, extended family, illness. The list of what can change our focus goes on and on. I'm confident I have left out many things, but you get the idea. Just as in a marriage relationship, our actions toward God reveal our focus.

Additionally, relationship woes cause love to cool. As a counselor and teacher, I could walk you through layers of topics that affect relationships.

There are listening skills or lack of them, expressive and receptive communication patterns, love languages, how to fill one another's love tank, and the like. The list can grow lengthy, but basically, it comes down to priority. The bottom line is that the relationship becomes less of a focus and other priorities take their place.

And here is the sad part. All too often, the participants are unaware of this cooling of love, the failure to put love first, and the resulting detriment to the relationship. Instead, they perceive everything as okay and still as good as it once was. And that, my friends, is deception.

Comfortable Christians have a respectable list of activities for particular circumstances and life events. They attend weddings and funerals. They show up for baby showers and graduations, birthday and anniversary celebrations, and the like. They teach Sunday School classes and sing in the choir. Excellent for sure, but those activities often become rote, mundane, meaningless, or worse: expected, which reflects ingratitude—obligation versus sincerity. We check off the boxes with little thought or effort. Isn't this exactly happened to Angie and David? Activities for the niceties of life somehow lost their zest, and the true motivation of their hearts no longer focused on the main thing: relationship. I've used the word comfort in describing this situation, but more realistically, the term should be disconnection! There are plenty of examples where *comfort* is not only acceptable but desirable, but disconnection and the lack of intimacy it reflects is not! How often do we do that with God? Once our love for the Father and the sacrifice of His Son Jesus was our prime motivation. We wanted to talk *about* Him with others, and we wanted to talk *to* Him. Reading and studying the Word was our way to spend time *with* Him, and we longed for and sought out intimacy that only He could fulfill in us through the presence of the Holy Spirit. But like our friends above, the motivation for our actions is no longer motivated by the desire to show our love, to embrace our fellowship with the one we love, and merely becomes a habit. A good habit, perhaps, but a habit nonetheless.

Here is a word of reflection. As we continue, we

will look at other fictional *scenarios* and see people whose behaviors you may identify with as you consider your heart condition. I hope you do not see yourself on these pages, and I encourage you to guard against only seeing others in these vignettes. But if you do see yourself, *hooray*! You have recognized a place from which to grow. And growth is always a good thing!

### HOW DO WE RENEW OUR FIRST LOVE?

1. **Talk to God about it and admit you were wrong.** Repent for letting other things take first place in your life. Confess losing track of your love for God. Just as in a marriage, love for God is a choice you make, a commitment that needn't be based on feelings, although feelings are undoubtedly present. Purpose in your heart to do better and to make amends. Rededicate your heart and your life to Jesus and commit to loving and honoring and serving Him.

2. **Get to know the character of God the**

**Father.** Jesus demonstrated the Father's love to us while He was on the earth. The more we get to know Jesus through reading how he lived and what He did, the better we understand the heart of the Father. When we get to know the Father, it is easy to be loyal to Him and depend on Him to help us navigate our lives here on earth. When you know you can trust someone, it is effortless for love to grow. The bible says that we love Him because He first loved us. Love will overwhelm us when we learn that we are accepted and cherished by the One who created us.

3. **Learn to hear from the Father with spiritual ears.** God wants to reveal Himself to us and to show us things to come. He wants to help us avoid pitfalls as we navigate a fallen world with "many toils and snares!" We learn to hear from Him through reading and studying the Word of God and through the Holy Spirit living in us. When we make Jesus our Lord and our Savior,

our spirits are made new, and the old man is dead and gone. We are alive in Christ! And Christ in us is the hope of glory and glorious living! Jesus came that we would have life and have it more abundantly. That means that there is always enough—more than enough. Tune your spiritual ears to hear all that God would say to you.

4. **Rejoice!** God will renew the joy of your salvation! And then moving forward with the Lord will be exciting and fulfilling! Psalms 51:12 says, *"Restore to me the joy of Your salvation, and uphold me by Your generous Spirit."* That's a good word. However, when we read it in The Passion Translation, the verse comes alive and resonates within our hearts and spirits: *"Let my passion for life be restored tasting joy in every breakthrough you bring to me. Hold me close to you with a willing spirit that obeys whatever you say."*

5. **Do The Next Thing.**

Chapter Three

# A WORD ABOUT LUKEWARM CHRISTIANS

Let's meet our next friends. Christine and Tommy are a couple you'll regularly see in church. Oh, they might miss if there is a big family event happening or if they decide to head out to the three-day-week-end antique show, but they are usually in church, on time, and looking great. They have never brought anyone to church with them, although they have neighbors they love and interact with and have family living nearby. Their children attended church with them while they were younger, but now that they are teens, Christine and Tommy want them to make their own decisions and no longer require them to come as a family. When their son TJ got in trouble for smoking weed at school, they let the administration handle it, although they had suspected some alcohol and drug use by him themselves. They just thought it might be better for TJ if they didn't make a huge deal of the incident.

Tommy is a friendly and outgoing guy, he gets along well with everybody, both those he works with and neighbors alike, and his circle of friends is mainly folks with similar incomes and interests. Tommy has stated that he doesn't want to offend anyone or make them uncomfortable by talking about church and God-stuff, so those topics never come up. And if they do, Tommy is very adept at steering the conversation back to safer ground. He prides himself on getting along with anyone, although he sometimes feels a bit concerned with his business partner, who has a gambling problem. But Jeff's a good guy, and Tommy doesn't want it to embarrass him by bringing it up.

Christine is a stay-at-home mom who is involved with her kids' school activities and likes to attend the ladies' functions at church. She also belongs to a Bunco Club with several acquaintances, and it makes her laugh to see how rambunctious a few gals can become over a few glasses of wine and a silly game. However, she smiles a lot and doesn't want to burden anyone when she faces a problem at home. And she certainly doesn't want to rock the boat when controversial topics come up. Christine is very proud of Tommy's success and enjoys seeing his name on the banners at Little League, where he has sponsored a team each year for decades. She realizes that they truly have everything they need and most of what they want, and she likes that. Tommy has provided well for their family.

The couple tries to vote in every election but rarely discusses the candidates or what they stand for. They just pick a familiar name or take friends' recommendations which may have mentioned a particular candidate. Neither Tommy nor Christine is sure why the whole abortion position is focused on so much by church friends when that is not even the issue in most elections. (Besides, their neighbor's daughter had an abortion a few years back, and she's okay. So what's the big deal?)

They are a successful couple living in both social and emotional bubbles. And they are comfortable.

## WHAT WENT WRONG?

I hope that when you read this last vignette, alarm bells went off in your head! Tommy and Christine are solid examples of lukewarm Christianity! They wish, they wash – they're wishy-washy. They stand for nothing. How does that old saying go? When you stand for nothing, you'll fall for anything? These two are in jeopardy of being greatly deceived. In fact, they are living in deception already. And because of their lack of conviction for the things of God, they are perfect prey for an enemy who wants nothing better than to gobble them up and spit them out! And the devil is not the only one. In Revelation, John tells what he heard Jesus say to the angel of the church of Laodicea, regarding lukewarm believers. *"So then, because you are lukewarm, and neither hot nor cold, I will vomit you out of My mouth"* (Revelation 3:16).

Being uncommitted is reprehensible to our Lord. When He spoke about the other churches in Revelation, he did not say he would *"spew them out."*. Not the loveless, compromised, corrupt, or even the dead. Nope, the *mugwumps* captured that flag all by themselves. They are the ones with their *"mugs"* on one side of the fence and their *"wumps"* on the other!

Those who follow Jesus only on their terms put themselves at risk. Dallying on a tightrope of yay or nay, those believers sway with indecision and non-committal lifestyles that ignore the promises of God. With reckless abandon, they teeter indiscriminately between righteousness and folly, faith and foolishness, and leave their hearts wide open for an enemy who wants to destroy them. Romans 1:21 admonishes, *"...although they knew God, they did not glorify Him as God, nor were they thankful, but became futile in their thoughts and their foolish hearts were darkened"* (NKJV). The same verse in The Passion Translation put it this way, *"This left them with nothing but misguided hearts, steeped in moral darkness. Although claiming to be wise, they were in fact shallow fools."*

> *"Having no true conviction for the things of God, no zest, leaves us bankrupt of spiritual values, for without any feeling of guilt, we lean this way or that and never settle on a course of godliness."*

Having no true conviction for the things of God, no zest, leaves us bankrupt of spiritual values, for without any feeling of guilt, we lean this way or that and never settle on a course of godliness. It is a waywardness allowing us to drift into whatever may come along, and if there are obstacles to overcome, we may find ourselves clinging to any available rescue offered. That, my friends, is dangerous territory!

Another danger is ignoring sin in our lives. When we don't recognize sin because we don't know God's Word well enough to define it, or when we cannot (or will not) hear the Holy Spirit when He brings conviction, we stand on slippery ground. Lack of sin-consciousness is often born of self-sufficiency. Therefore, it is imperative that we honestly and regularly evaluate our actions and make the necessary adjustments.

All too often, people fall into the trap of feeling everything is okay, well, because everything *is* okay. But valuing worldly wealth, status, and a life of ease is no replacement for acknowledging God as our source and provider. It is easy to slip away from our relationship with God when we feel there is no need for Him in our lives. A *ho-hum* desire for connection with Him is a significant symptom of living lukewarm.

## HOW DO WE AVOID BECOMING LUKEWARM?

1. **Acknowledge areas in your life that are tepid.** Repent for allowing enthusiasm for the things of God to wane. Stir yourself up!

2. **Value the true riches of kingdom living (righteousness, peace, and joy) above worldly success, wealth, or assets.** Hold on to the things with spiritual value. Keep the main thing the *main thing*! Jesus!

3. **Establish a spiritual value system and make it a priority in your life.** "What would Jesus do?" is a pretty good filter by which to check your decisions. Establish relationships with godly friends who will offer you accountability as you commit to redirecting your focus.

4. **Do the Next Thing.**

## Chapter Four

# A WORD ABOUT COMPROMISED CHRISTIANS

Walt and Barbara are empty nesters. Only one of their three children is married, and they are anxiously awaiting grandchildren. None of the kids live close by, but they try to get together for the holidays. Walt still works part-time at the job he has had for over 30 years and plays golf with co-workers from time to time. He enjoys the time with the "boys," who often tell a lewd joke or two, and they always end up at the 19th Hole. He also loves football and has a good time when his neighbors host parties nearly every weekend during the fall. There is usually a keg or other mixed drinks. Guests often drink a little too much, but Walt doesn't pay much attention. Walt does drink a bit himself, mostly to fit in and not be the odd man out. However, one time one of the college kids brought some marijuana to share, he just laughed and waved off their offer, but he felt pretty uncomfortable. Walt didn't want to make a scene and stayed quiet. He also stayed at the party.

Barb is no longer staying home to be a mom, she's just staying home. She enjoys projects around the house and has redecorated the kids' rooms to be more guest-friendly. Her craft projects occupy some of her time, as does shopping, but honestly, she is a bit bored. She took her friend's recommendation about her favorite soap operas, and Barb now spends a couple of hours a day watching them. She and her friend get a kick discussing all the crazy problems the daytime drama characters find themselves in repeatedly. They also started a yoga class a few months ago, and their instructor gave them crystals to hang on the mirrors in their cars for "peace and serenity." Barb is thinking about getting another one. She found a really pretty one labeled "health and harmony" at her favorite gift shop, and it matches her kitchen perfectly.

The couple attends church, but they haven't volunteered anywhere since the kids were in youth group, when they hosted social events at their home. Walt once signed up to be an usher but found it challenging to be at church 45 minutes before service started. They considered attending a home group a few months ago, but there wasn't a group meeting near them that had a convenient schedule. They are comfortable financially and willingly write a check to a good cause when asked to do so. However, they prefer not to get personally involved with those recipients. They never consider serving at the local food bank or dropping off diapers at the local crisis pregnancy center, but they often donate money to each. No one knows that Walt financed his former girlfriend's abortion while in college, not even Barb, and frankly, Walt has pretty much forgotten all about it himself.

They consider themselves open-minded and try to be accepting of those they encounter who live alternative lifestyles. They believe that even if they disagree with someone or something, it is better to be quiet. After all, Jesus taught to *"turn the other cheek,"* right?

## WHAT WENT WRONG?

How many red flags regarding walking the Christian walk could you spot here? There are lots. Most of all, I see that both Walt and Barbara have allowed little things to creep in and move them off the path of righteousness.

Let's consider that path of righteousness as parallel lines, like a railroad track. Father God, the Creator of the universe and the One who loves us unconditionally, has laid out His standards for us to navigate this life here on earth. I mean, who knows better how to accomplish the desired purpose than the One who made everything anyway? In His great love for us, He has not made those standards a rule book that we are invited to follow. Remember, the Israelites tried that already, unsuccessfully! Instead, He has set forth guidelines that will ensure our success *if* we follow them. And He has provided a written manual to consult when we face difficulty, the B-I-B-L-E, *Basic Instructions Before Leaving Earth!* Better yet, He also left tech support which we can access 24/7, the Holy Spirit! One of my favorite verses is Isaiah 30, verse 21. Check this out: *"Your ears shall hear a word behind you, saying 'This is the way, walk in it,' whenever you turn to the right hand or whenever you turn to the left."* So, we have a guideline, the Bible, and it is available in several excellent translations that make it comprehendible for every reader. And we have a Guide! That's God's side of the track.

Our part in traveling this railroad track of righteousness is to align ourselves with the Word of God and make our decisions for daily living, not by some legalistic requirement, but rather in obedience to a loving father, Who wants to guard and protect His children. Here's the problem that believers often face, which can throw them off the track or even lead to their destruction: they do not know what is in the guidebook or do not know the Guide. There is more.

> *"Here's the problem that believers often face, which can throw them off the track or even lead to their destruction: they do not know what is in the guidebook or do not know the Guide."*

When Christians rely on their upbringing, opinion, education, or experience to determine what is *right* or *good,* we get ourselves into trouble. The Bible says that *"all our righteousness acts are like filthy rags"* (Isaiah 64:6). So, when we veer away from the path God has graciously provided for us to follow, we fail Him and open ourselves up to unwanted consequences even if only a little bit. Veering from the right path is what happened to Walt and

Barbara.

They got a bit off track with their thinking. Maybe Walt and Barbara didn't even notice that they were not aligned with God at first. Serving God became a bit inconvenient, so they went for the easy route. Their focus was off-kilter, and they used a world standard for what was acceptable. Then they just ignored the errors rather than repenting and adjusting their thoughts and behaviors to what would please God. And after they ignored their errors (sin), it was easy to deny their mistakes (sin). Walt and Barb slipped even more and began to partake of what was not in God's plan, a lewd joke, too many drinks, gossip, toying with spirituality that was not godly. They even went so far as to believe that they were living and what they thought was God-ordained. They were satisfied in their actions and their beliefs and saw no reason to change. They thought they were comfortable, but what they were was comprised. And they were deceived.

Compromised believers are nothing new. We are in the last days, and Timothy warned us what would happen. Yet, 2 Timothy 3:1—6 is challenging to read. Why? Because we recognize the signs of the times in it.

*"But know this, that in the last days perilous times will come: for men will be lovers of themselves, lovers of money, boasters, proud, blasphemers, disobedient to parents, unthankful, unholy, unloving, unforgiving, slanderers, without self-control, brutal, despisers of good, traitors, headstrong, haughty, lovers of pleasure rather than lovers of God, having a form of godliness but denying its power. And from such people turn away!"*

It is a very slippery slope from comfortable to compromise. There are ungodly things nearly everywhere we look. Movies advertise sin in overt ways, and not just the R-rated ones. Likewise, the PG-13 topics can be toxic and immoral drawing us away from what God would have us focus on daily. That *"parental guidance"* label is important for parents, not just kids! And tell me what justification any sold-out believer would have for watching an R-rated movie? Yes, I know this is a hard line, but compromise begins with accepting the little things that are not quite right! Let's look at Philippians 4:8, a familiar verse, but one that is not always adhered to: *"Finally brethren, whatever things are true, whatever things are noble, whatever things are just, whatever things are pure, whatever things are lovely, whatever things are of good report, if there is any virtue and if there is anything praiseworthy, meditate on these things."*

When we look at the verse from The Passion Translation, I believe God's intention for our thought life, and subsequently, our behavior is clear. *"Keep your thoughts continually fixed on all that is authentic and real, honorable and admirable, beautiful and respectful, pure and holy, merciful and kind. And fasten your thoughts on every glorious work of God, praising him always."* Being willing to live by that one verse alone will help you avoid compromise in many areas of your life. And that is only one single verse from the *"guidebook"* that is provided to help you live in righteousness, peace, and joy.

# HOW DO WE FIND RESTORATON AFTER COMPROMISE?

1. **Guard that you never renounce Jesus.** Be aware of worldly enticements that draw you away from seeking God as your only source for godliness, peace, and satisfaction. Ask the Holy Spirit to speak to you and guide you.

2. **Identify any part of your life that is off track and repent.** Do not settle or be okay with less than what would please God. Understand that being just a little bit off today will lead to significant error down the road. If you are unsure, check it out in the Word, meanwhile, "When in doubt, leave it out!"

3. **Study the "guidebook" to quickly know how God has taught us to live.** The Word of God is the only standard by which we should evaluate our thoughts, beliefs, and our actions. Proverbs is an excellent book to find wisdom.

**4. Learn to hear from the Holy Spirit.** Recognize the voice of God from the written Word, from godly teaching, and communication with the Spirit of God. His is a voice that will never lead you off track. The more we know of the character and ways of God, the less likely we will fall into compromise.

**5. Do The Next Thing.**

# Chapter Five

# A Word About Corrupt Christians

Ed is well-known among his community and enjoys terrific name recognition, probably because he ran for City Council a few years back and lost by only a few votes in a fiery run-off.

He considers himself a *"big dog"* and serves as a board member for several charitable associations. He owns a business, employing several dozen people, and has been financially successful and tends to equate that success with goodness and superiority. Ed found a great tax attorney who sees all the loopholes and is only partly joking when he tells Ed to pray that they don't get audited.

Ed prides himself on running a tight ship, and often when employees come to him to share a need or request time off, Ed is dismissive and doesn't want to hear it. He usually allows them time off but often docks their pay even if they try to explain the situation to him. Larry is one of his workers. Larry's son was in a bad car accident and required a lengthy hospitalization, but Ed was disinterested to the point of rudeness. His bottom line for personnel is, "Just do your job. I will do mine."

Ed was married for several years, but his extramarital affair a few years back destroyed his marriage, although he tells anyone who will listen that it was his wife's fault. He vows he will never marry again but is considering asking the woman he's been dating for the past three years to move in with him. Ed goes to church most of the time, albeit less since his divorce. He did help plan and fund the new church fellowship hall and liked seeing his name on the cornerstone where supporters are listed. He knows a few verses that he remembers from being a kid but really isn't too interested in Bible study. God has already made him successful. What more could he need?

## WHAT WENT WRONG?

This chapter about Ed should never have had to be written about Christians. In Revelation, Paul wrote about the corrupt church in Thyatira. The people were morally bankrupt, just like Ed. They were believers who simply got of track and allowed themselves to lose sight of what Jesus had taught and demonstrated to them through his actions.

Today some believers have met Jesus sometime in their life and accepted Him, having their spirits reborn within them but somehow fell away. In 2 Thessalonians, Chapter 2, Paul writes about a great falling away, sometimes referred to as the Great Apostasy. According to Paul, this departure from the truth is a necessary step before Jesus returns and verse 3 opens with a warning regarding it, *"Let no one deceive you by any means."* Unfortunately, this chapter topic includes the organized church and individual pastors who have not only gone astray but have led others down an evil path. Or worse, maliciously harmed anyone who disagreed or attempted to shed light on the evil they perpetrated. But this book is not for pastors or even church leadership. God will deal with them in

> *"This book is for believers who have been lured off the path of righteousness by an enemy that wants to destroy them."*

His time and in His way. This book is for believers who have been lured off the path of righteousness by an enemy that wants to destroy them. And without repentance and turning away from evil, destruction is sure to come.

It is unlikely that you will see yourself in this vignette, primarily because someone who has fallen away and abandoned God to corruption would probably never pick up this book, much less read it! But the warning is still one to consider. How does one become *"dead"*? (And I'm not talking Zombie Apocalypse here!)

Paul writes about immature believers who once again need to be taught the basics of faith. From his words in Hebrews 5:12, we understand that we can receive teaching yet *"lose it"* requiring those lessons to be taught again so that we can grow and mature in our Christian walk. While we will discuss how believers lose ground in their faith walk, in this chapter on the corrupt Christian, these principles apply to each of the vignettes in this book.

Jesus taught the Parable of the Seed and the Sower, which is recounted in three of the four gospels. You can read it and its explanation in Matthew 13, Mark 4, and Luke 8. Jesus taught about how the Word of God slips away from us, and therefore fails to produce life change because the Word is not in us. Let's look at what He taught.

Jesus describes the seed as the Word of God and the ground that it is planted in as the soil of man's heart. The first example is where the seed is sown on the wayside. The wayside is the edge of a road, slightly off the trodden path. Here is a definition from *dictionary.com.*

*"The seed sown by the wayside represents the Word of God as it falls upon the heart of the inattentive hearer. As the birds catch the seed from the wayside, satan catches away the seeds of divine truth from the soul. Satan knows that the Word of God may awaken the careless and take effect upon the hardened heart."* That's a pretty good definition. The Bible says that the devil comes and takes the Word out of the believer's heart, and although he hears the Word, he doesn't understand it or ignores it, so the wicked one quickly snatches away what should have been sown in the believer's heart. The seed fails to produce because it is stolen.

The second scenario is when the seed of the Word of God is sown on rocky soil. The believer hears and receives the Word with joy and believes for a while. But because no root can be established on the hard ground, he does not endure when temptation or persecution arises because of the Word, and he falls away. This believer without good roots immediately stumbles when there is a season of difficulty or harassment by the enemy. Here is where I fear many Christians are today. They once received the Word with gladness and failed to have it take root. The last days are upon us, and Jesus said that things would get tough before His return, and without deep roots, it will be easy to stumble and fall away. God forbid!

The following example presents the seed that fell among thorns. In this case, the believer heard the Word, but, as he went out into the world, that Word in his heart was choked out by the cares, riches, and pleasures of life, subsequently bringing no fruit to maturity. It's otherwise described as anxious care, the deceitfulness of riches, and desires for the fleeting pleasures of this life. We live in pressure-filled times, and it is easy to be burdened with financial woes, relationship difficulties, and the seemingly unending pursuit of affluence. And everywhere we look, we see advertisements selling us the *"fleeting pleasures of life."* First John 2:15-17 brings both warning and encouragement. *"Do not love the world or the things that are in the world. If anyone loves the world, the love of the Father is not in him. For all that is in the world--the lust of the flesh, the lust of the eyes, and the pride of life--is not of the Father but is of the world. And the world is passing away, and the lust of it; but he who does the will of God abides forever."*

Abiding with God forever and living in righteousness, peace, and joy is only accomplished by taking heed to the Word of God, hiding it in our hearts, and applying it daily to our lives.

## HOW DO WE AVOID BECOMING CORRUPT?

1. **Hear the Word and guard your heart with all diligence to keep it.** Do not let the enemy steal it. Allow it to take root and bear

fruit in your life. Do not let the truth be overshadowed by worries, striving for earthly riches, or craving pleasures that lead you astray. Be sober, be diligent.

2. **Reject any teaching or practice that lures you away from godliness.** Avoid sexual immorality, especially.

3. **Recognize when and where you falter. Be quick to repent.** Make a plan to avoid that area of temptation. Refusing to repent and turn away from sin is destructive both to you and to those who love you.

4. **Do not keep company with others who are not heeding the truth of the Word of God.** While this seems harsh, it is for your growth and protection. The Bible says to not even share a meal with those who practice corruption. Separating yourself to God is a good thing. It is sanctification.

5. **Establish and sustain a strong relationship with God through the presence of the Holy Spirit in your life.** Listen to the voice behind you, which will whisper, *"This is the way, walk in it."*

Develop your spiritual prayer language. Commit daily to be a sold-out Christ-follower.

**6. Do The Next Thing.**

Chapter Six

# A WORD ABOUT
# DEAD CHRISTIANS

Reshay and Carter represent yet another group of comfortable Christians. They go to church, but they stay in their small group. Even outside of the church, they have little interaction with people who are different than them. Carter is friendly and likable and is quick to say, "I'll pray for you," yet somehow, it doesn't really happen. Or sometimes he says what I call the *"God Bless You"* prayers, which basically means he tosses someone's name up into the air, hoping it will reach the ears of God and have some effect. Unfortunately, he cannot remember a specific time when he prayed and got actual results.

Reshay works full-time in a job that she likes but finds it a bit less than fulfilling. However, the money is good and allows her to buy the fun things she wants for her family, nice birthday gifts or new home decorations, and even occasionally a weekend trip out of town.

Reshay has a habit of complaining about what is happening around her and exudes an attitude of *"ain't it awful."* She tends to rate circumstances near her as better or worse than her situation, and while she doesn't always voice her assessment, it is a constant idea in her thoughts. She considers herself *"in the know"* because she spends a lot of time on the phone with her friends from church or work and knows what is happening in the lives of those folks she knows in the community. Reshay tends to look at her friends or neighbors comparing what is happening in their lives to her own. It comforts her to think, *"Well, at least I'm not doing THAT!"* The truth is that Reshay is not doing much of anything, but instead is wrapped up in a blanket of self-satisfaction, and she is cozy in it.

Every year Carter and Reshay send out dozens of Christmas cards and receive dozens as well. Reshay asks Carter to help her since a large part of the list is his business associates, but he reminds her that his *"help"* is buying the cards and stamps. So every year, the list gets longer, and Reshay declares that next year she will have them printed with their signatures. But Reshay tackles the job anyway and tries to get the cards out early, so if someone wants to reciprocate with a card to them, they will have plenty of time to do so.

Neither Reshay nor Carter can remember a specific time when they gave their hearts to the Lord, but they aren't much concerned about that because they know that deep down, they are good people and that they care about the right things. They, too, are comfortable.

## WHAT WENT WRONG?

The truth is Carter and Reshay are *too* comfortable. They say and do the right things however they're numb to the things of God. Their good reputation and friendly actions have lulled them to sleep. They function, but not with the life of God in them. They are dead spiritually. Being spiritually dead actually leaves us *about* God but *without* God. Paul wrote about spiritually dead believers in his second letter to Timothy, in which he discussed perilous times. Second Timothy 3: 5 & 7: *"They pretend to have a respect for God but in reality, they want nothing to do with God's power. Stay away from people like these! They are always learning but never discover the revelation-knowledge of truth"* (TPT). The New King James Version states, *"Always learning but never able to come to the knowledge of the truth."*

This passage perfectly describes the information age in which we live today. Paul describes those Christians who maintain a great outward appearance. They use Christian lingo and do Christian behaviors (like sending Christmas cards) but do not live in the reality of what authentic Christian faith produces. They deny the power of God to work in them. The power that is central to our faith. Power exuding from the truth of a risen Savior, the validity of the God-breathed Word, and the inpouring and outflowing presence of the Holy Spirit, who works within each believer's heart to effect change and radically transform lives. Caution: The Bible says we should stay away from those powerless people! Without revelation knowledge of God, all spiritual growth will cease, and eventually, the sham of their beliefs and actions will be revealed. We will be peering into spiritual coffins housing dead believers! In his comments on Revelation, Jack Hayford succinctly

> *"Without revelation knowledge of God, all spiritual growth will cease, and eventually, the sham of their beliefs and actions will be revealed. We will be peering into spiritual coffins housing dead believers!"*

states what we need to remember. *"Outward works do not always indicate a right heart, but a right heart condition always produces good works."*

In Matthew, Jesus is teaching the crowd what has become known as the Sermon on the Mount. His wisdom covers many topics over three chapters. First, let's read Matthew 7:21—23:

*"Not everyone who says to me, 'Lord, Lord,' shall enter the kingdom of heaven, but he who does the will of My Father in heaven. Many will say to me in that day, 'Lord, Lord, have we not prophesied in Your name, cast out demons in Your name, and done many wonders in Your name?' And then I will declare to them, 'I never knew you; depart from Me you who practice lawlessness'"* (NKJV).

That is a sobering statement: *"Depart from me. I never knew you."* Wow! Even though Carter and Reshay were not frontline demonstrators of Christian power and authority, prophesying or casting out demons, their lackluster *"good"* behavior was not in obedience to the will of the

Father. They simply go through the motions of what they think Christians should do, but without any real connection to God. Will Jesus accept their superficial actions, or will Carter and Reshay hear those devastating words? *I never knew you.*

Jesus further teaches what happens to those who do not apply the Words of the Lord in the verses that follow. Matthew 27:24-27 in The Passion Translation reads this way: *"Everyone who hears my teaching and applies it to his life can be compared to a wise man who built his house on an unshakable foundation. When the rains fell and the flood came, with fierce winds beating upon his house, it stood firm because of its strong foundation. But everyone who hears my teaching and does not apply it to his life can be compared to a foolish man who built his house on sand. When it rained and rained and the flood came, with wind and waves beating upon his house, it collapsed and was swept away."*

Here again, is the warning: If we do not adhere to His instructions and cling to our relationship with Jesus when storms and trials come (and they will!), our foundation will wash away and not sustain us. Our house will be washed away; our shelter, protection, comfort, and peace will be gone. But we have hope when we cling to Jesus!

## HOW DO WE AVOID BEING "DEAD" CHRISTIANS?

Again, we quote Jack Hayford (from the Spirit-filled Life Bible, Truth-in-Action for Revelation):

1. **Listen to what the Spirit is saying.** Tune your ear to hear through the Word of God, sound teaching, and from the Holy Spirit.
2. **When forced to choose, obey God, not man.** Those decisions may be big ones that are easily recognized; however, those small daily decisions can mar your faith walk if you falter in them.
3. **Do not be lulled to sleep because of a good reputation.** Do not think too highly

of yourself but rather walk in humility and submit to the will of God.

4. **Keep pressing into Jesus.** Daily Bible reading and hearing good teaching is paramount to keeping alive your relationship with Jesus.

5. **Make sure you practice the teaching you have received.** Avoid being a hearer only, lest you deceive yourself.

6. **Obey God's Word to YOU.** It matters not what others are doing. *Your* role is to obey what God asks of *you*.

7. **Do the Next Thing.**

Chapter Seven

# A WORD ABOUT DANGER

As we get down to the wire in what I believe are the *"last days,"* let's get real for a minute. Face it: there are dozens of books coming out every day telling us how bad things are. And frankly, there *are* many things in our world today that are not great. But I decided that if I presented descriptions of what needs to change, I would also bring suggestions for my readers to learn how to improve their own lives. I knew I had to focus on what specific outcomes I desired for my readers, for YOU! Additionally, I want to share the explicit warnings the Bible presents regarding the dangers we face as The Day approaches. Keep in mind that these are not *my* warnings but come straight from the Word of God!

> *"Anytime we are out of the will of God, it is a crisis! The time before Jesus returns for us will be difficult. I want you to be spiritually ready to face the hard stuff without losing hope, faith, or giving up."*

Why did I include warnings? Because I hope that none of you experience the crisis of faith that we saw in the believers we met earlier. Anytime we are out of the will of God, it is a crisis! However, when we look again at Matthew 24, we see that the time before Jesus returns for us will be difficult. That time is fast approaching! I want you to be spiritually ready to face the hard stuff without losing hope, faith, or giving up.

Many of our parents and grandparents went through tough times. World War I, a flu pandemic in the 1920s that killed thousands, the Great Depression, and World War II caused upheaval in their lives like they had never experienced. Many had minimal material goods, and life was indeed a struggle. Many lost loved ones. And many had a crisis of faith during that time, losing both their hope and trust in God.

Just as The Weather Channel presents us with explicit warnings about a coming snowstorm or hurricane so that we can prepare, so also the Bible offers up a warning so that we can prepare for possible disaster. We have lived comfortably in our blessed and affluent society for decades, and most of us have never truly had a life-threatening challenge. Even the poorest among us usually have access to medical treatment, food supplies, shelter, transportation, and, more often than not, telephone and television. Fully stocked shelves in stores, utility services, and communication technology are seldom unavailable. A severe disruption of services or delivery of goods may cause a crisis of supply and a crisis of faith. You've probably read, or even studied, some end-time theology. You know, "...*wars and rumors of war, nations against nations, famines, pestilences (plagues), and earthquakes*" (Matthew 24:6&7). These are things we have little control over as individuals.

My concern follows in verses 10, 11, & 12. Here Jesus says, "*And then many will be offended, betray one another, and will hate one another. Then many false prophets will rise up and deceive many. And because lawlessness will abound, the love of many will grow cold.*"

He is not describing the unsaved people on the street, though they will experience this as well. He is talking about Christians—believers sitting in church and yet, falling away. Jesus gave us a heads up, a warning.

Amos also gave a warning that applies today in Chapter 8, verse 11: "*Behold, the days are coming,*" says the Lord God, "*that I will send a famine on the land, not a famine of bread, nor thirst for water,* **but of hearing the words of the Lord**" (Emphasis mine). In *The Spirit-Filled Life Bible,* Jack Hayford's commentary about this verse explains, *"no assurance will be available that God has heard their cry for help. No direction from God will guide them in their times of need. All will be silent."*

This verse and warning occurred in the Old Testament (old covenant), and of course, since we are living under the new covenant, we have the indwelling of the Holy Spirit. But if we get off track following false teachers, or worse, fail even to bother *trying* to hear the voice of the Lord, we have no more advantage than those in the days of old who could not hear from God for themselves. Eleanor Roosevelt once wrote, *"A man who does not read is no better off than one who can't."* My daughters had heard me say that a lot and delighted in changing it up whenever possible to tease me. Like, *a woman who does not do dishes is no better off than one who can't.* (I think that was funnier in my head! But my kids made me laugh!)

If we apply that logic to the idea of hearing from God through the Bible and the Holy Spirit, it is easy to see that we could quickly become just like those who do not know God at all. We live in a time where there may indeed be a famine of hearing the words of the Lord!

Perhaps you are familiar with 2 Timothy 3:1—9, Paul describes those perilous times. The word *perilous* describes a *"society that is barren of virtue but abounding with vices. Harsh, savage, difficult, dangerous, painful, fierce, grievous, hard to deal with"* (Strong's Concordance #5467). Yet another definition is *"raging insanity."* Again, Jack Hayford's commentary in *The Spirit-filled Life Bible* is clear. *"People will be characterized by all kinds of self-centered and unnatural perversions. Some will maintain an outward pretense, speaking the vocabulary of Christianity but refusing the reality that the Christian faith expresses. The power they deny is the heart of Christianity--the fact of a risen Redeemer, the truth of the inspired Word, and the indwelling and overflowing of the Holy Spirit working within believers and transforming their lives."*

Let's continue. I could write it no more clearly than it is presented in The Passion Translation. Let's read 2 Timothy 3:1—9. *"But you need to be aware that in the final days the culture of society will become extremely fierce. People will be self-centered lovers of themselves and obsessed with money. They will boast of great things as they strut around in their arrogant pride and mock all that is right. They will ignore their own families. They will be ungrateful and ungodly. They will become addicted to hateful and malicious slander. Slaves to their desires, they will be ferocious, belligerent haters of what is good and right. With brutal treachery they will act without restraint, bigoted and wrapped in clouds of their conceit. They will find their delight in pleasures of this world more than pleasures of the loving God. They may pretend to have a respect for God, but in reality, they want nothing to do with God's power. Stay away from people like these! For they are the ones who wormed their way into the hearts of vulnerable women, a spending the night with those who are captured by their lust and steeped in sin. They are always learning but never discover the revelation knowledge of the truth. So it will be in the last days with those who reject the faith with their corrupt minds and arrogant hearts, standing against the truth of God. But they will not advance for everyone will see their madness..."*

The perfect description of dangerous territory. Why? Because unless you are carefully guarding your heart, you might fall prey to the same treachery that deceived them!

First Timothy 4:1 & 2 continues this description of the end-time deception and apostasy. *"Now the Spirit expressly says that in latter times some will depart from the faith giving heed to deceiving spirits and doctrines of demons speaking lies in hypocrisy having in their own conscience seared with a hot iron." "Apostasy"* simply means *that some will deny the essential doctrines of Christianity!* The deceiving spirits and doctrines of demons will draw many away through the teaching of perverse ideas, often presented as political correctness. We are urged in First John 4:1 to test (examine, discern, prove) the spirits and do not believe everything you hear or read on the internet!! Verse 2 from The Passion Translation tells us how to test them. *"Here's the test for those with genuine spirit of God: They will confess Jesus as the Christ who has come in the flesh. Everyone who does not acknowledge that Jesus is from God has the spirit of Antichrist which you heard was coming and is already active in the world."*

The admonishment continues in Hebrews 2:1. *"Therefore, we must give the more earnest heed to the things we have heard **lest we drift away.**"* *Emphasis mine.* Then another in Psalms 119: 9, *"How can a young man stay pure? Only by living in the Word of God and walking in its truth"* *(TPT).*

These are real dangers facing us as believers, and we must be ready to remain steadfast when these things come. Acknowledging that we are at risk is paramount. Remember, back in earlier chapters, we learned that a sign of complacency was an unwillingness to recognize or even care about the dangers that may be lurking outside our own purview. We will not be close-minded or blinded by a life of contentment, ease, or comfort.

First Corinthians 10: 12 from The Passion Translation says it all! *"So beware if you think it could never happen to you, lest your pride become your downfall."* So now what?

**Let's do the next thing!**

## Chapter Eight

# A WORD ABOUT THE PANDEMIC

Don't think for a minute that comfortable Christianity and the topics discussed here are a new thing. They are not new. What *is* new is what we experienced from the 2020 pandemic and its wretched impact on both the church and individual believers. Closed churches and isolation from fellow believers, well, from everyone, have caused the body of Christ great harm. The church body as a whole and its leaders have dealt with issues never before faced, and unfortunately, many have failed to lead well to bring us through this devasting time. Hebrews 10:25 admonishes us to gather together with God's people, our fellow believers, to be encouraged and urged on in our faith. The Passion Translation puts it like this: *"This is not the time to pull away and neglect meeting together, as some have formed the habit of doing. In fact, we should come together even more frequently, eager to encourage and urge each other as we anticipate that day dawning"*.

Not only have we been isolated from those who could encourage and exhort us, but many people have also experienced fear like never before. Fear of the unknown, fear of sickness, fear of death, fear for loved ones and the real possibility of losing them permanently, fear of isolation, fear of the result of economic impact through lost jobs, lost income, lost housing, and more.

Regardless of your political bent and extraordinary politicization of this pandemic, we must look at the vast spiritual concern and impact poured upon the earth. While no debate is necessary, we must recognize this fact: a far-reaching spirit of fear has touched and effectively immobilized billions of believers and non-believers alike.

Second Timothy 1:7 declares, *"For God has not given us a spirit of fear, but of a spirit of power, and of love, and a sound mind."* If you look at Strong's Concordance (# 4995), it describes the term sound mind as *"a combination of sos 'safe' and phren 'the mind.'"* Hence, safe thinking! Not only did the shutdown that resulted because of the pandemic spur enormous fear, but it also caused millions to lose their *"sound thinking."* Too many have been caught up in fear and without the benefit of a

> *"A far-reaching spirit of fear has touched and effectively immobilized billions of believers and non-believers alike. And, too many Christians shifted their vertical focus on faith in God to a horizontal direction on fear of the pandemic."*

sound mind! And we know from Scripture that God did not give us that spirit of fear. The enemy satan did and, in doing so, swung wide an open door to devasting deception. Far too many Christians shifted their vertical focus on faith in God to a horizontal direction on fear of the pandemic.

We live in a culture where news is available twenty-four hours a day, seven days a week. Long past is the days of one or two networks that brought us the information (alas, I'd like to say facts!) from which we could form our own opinions. Nowadays, it is difficult to find a network, or single broadcast for that matter, delivering information without a biased slant or political interest. We have learned that only 5 or 6 major corporations own about 90% of the media outlets, and media outlets are not in business for the people's good. They are businesses, *big* businesses, that exist to boost their bottom line. The profit margin is king! When one looks further and learns what type of corporations these are, you know how they make their money. It is easy to extrapolate that pharmaceutical companies make money from selling medications, not from selling health when you follow the money. There are many ways to research these ideas. This is not the avenue for me to purport the many viewpoints out there. I will tell you this, however. First Peter 5:8, 9 warns: *"Be sober, be vigilant, because your adversary the devil walks about like a roaring lion, seeking whom he may devour. Resist him, steadfast in the faith knowing that the same sufferings are experienced by your brotherhood in the world."*

Sober here means *self-controlled*, and vigilant means *watchful*. We must not allow others to control us or our thinking. We bear a responsibility to obtain truthful information on which to base our decisions. Not only regarding the pandemic and its issues, but in all things as we go through life and face hard places. And we must be watchful to what is happening around us so that we are not surprised by an enemy who wants to destroy us. Jesus speaks to us in John 10:10: *"The thief does not come except to steal, kill, and destroy. I have come that they may have life, and that they may have it more abundantly."*

We can no longer be satisfied just to sit back and let others take the lead in every situation. We are instructed to be *"in* the world, not *of* the world," which does not mean that we ignore the world. We have an unction to carry the love of God to people (that means to *everybody!*), and we must know what others are facing to help them navigate life. Jesus told us that things would not be easy. In John 6:33, He says, *"In this world there will be tribulation. But be of good cheer. I have overcome the world."* Be armed with the weapons that God has provided us to use against the enemy. Be ready as good soldiers to deliver peace to a world in tribulation. And be of good cheer. We know how this is going to end! We win!

We must take care not to get sucked into emotional persuasion from those around us who want to sway our view to theirs. There are churches and pastors (some of them quite well known) taking a strong position and declaring that they have heard from God on the matters. I implore you not to be sheep but to search out the issue before God and make your decisions regarding your personal health care. Proverb 25:2 says, *"It is the glory of God to conceal a matter, but the glory of kings is to search it out a matter."* Look at the same scripture from The Passion Translation: *"God conceals the revelation of his Word in the hiding place of his glory. But the honor of kings is revealed by how they thoroughly search out the deeper meaning of all that God says."*

We are instructed to test the spirits and see if they are indeed from God. We must use the Bible filter to determine if what is being demanded of us would please God. Knowing God's character and His will is the only way to make decisions that best impact your life and the lives of your family. James 1:5 instructs us to ask God when we are uncertain of what to do. *"If any of you lacks wisdom let him ask of God, who gives to all liberally and without reproach, and it will be given to him."* Do not get caught up in emotional persuasion.

Charlana Kelly, the founder of Women of

Influence Network, explains emotional persuasion as coming from one who ministers to the soulish realm. Often that person only wants to change someone's mind to have them enjoin their opinions, not allowing freedom of choice for the one who is being influenced. Hitler used the love message of Christianity to manipulate the church during World War II. He portrayed himself as a Baptist and used the Bible to support his positions. Stalin so deceived the church that *thousands* made him their leader. Each of these men used a language of love, but we must know that the language of love and the language of seduction are very similar! And, it's imperative that we understand the power of truth spoken in love and be willing to be misunderstood and falsely accused as we recognize and call out emotional persuasion.

Significant damage occurred in the church about ten years ago when Pastor Rob Bell declared that if God is good, then there is no hell. While that is a "friendly" message, it is not true! It is unacceptable. When a weapon of "untruth" (a lie!) is deployed against believers, we *must* understand how to revoke it! Be aware! Love is being used to deceive and divide believers, and therefore the church. Pastors declaring *"Jesus would get vaccinated"* or *"If you really love your neighbor, you'd get vaccinated!"* is an example of emotional persuasion. Do you really believe that if Jesus, the Son of God Incarnate, were on earth today that he would NEED a vaccine? No! He would be healing all who were sick! We must learn to walk in the power of the Holy Spirit! I firmly believe that everyone should decide *whether to be vaccinated.* I am totally opposed to those who manipulate and force their beliefs on others. As believers, we must learn to hear the voice of God through the Holy Spirit and Word of God to make wise decisions for our daily lives. Again, the bottom line is, do you know God well enough to trust Him? Spoiler alert: We CAN trust Him!

Chapter Nine

# A WORD ABOUT THE GREAT COMMISSION

The purpose of this book is not to point out what is lacking but to stir and inspire readers to step up their faith and fulfill the call of God on their lives!

In Matthew 28, the letters in red tell us to go and make disciples of all the nations. Matthew 28:19 & 20 from The Passion Translation says, *"Now wherever you go make disciples of all nations, baptizing them in the name of the Father and of the Son and of the Holy Spirit. And teach them to faithfully follow all that I have commanded you. And never forget that I am with you every day even to the completion of the age."*

Jesus had come first to the Jews, but when He accomplished the work on The Cross, He offered His sacrificial gift of redemption to the whole world. God the Father desires that every person come to a saving knowledge of Jesus. The truth is we are not all called to be pastors. Nor are we all called to travel to foreign nations to preach the Gospel. However, we are each called to be evangelists and we've been given the ministry of reconciliation. Second Corinthians 5:18 & 20 says, *"And God has made all things new and reconciled us to Himself and given us the ministry of reconciling others to God. We are ambassadors of the Anointed One who carry the message of Christ to the world, as though God were tenderly pleading with them directly through our lips. So we tenderly plead with you on Christ's behalf, "Turn back to God and be reconciled to Him" (TPT).*

In Mark 16:15, Jesus appeared to the

remaining eleven disciples and said to them, *"Go into all the world and preach the gospel to every creature."* But wait, there's more!

*"And He said to them, 'As you go into all the world, preach openly the wonderful news of the gospel to the entire human race! Whoever believes the good news and is baptized will be saved and whoever does not believe the good news will be condemned. And these miracle signs will accompany those who believe. They will drive out demons in the power of my name. They will speak in tongues. They will be supernaturally protected from snakes and drinking anything poisonous. And they will lay hands on the sick and heal them'"* (Mark 16: 17-18 TPT).

Jesus also told the disciples of His great promise of the Holy Spirit. In Acts 1:8, he tells us, *"You shall receive power when the Holy Spirit has come upon you."* With the presence and power of the Holy Spirit, we can boldly and lovingly deliver the Good News of salvation! Jesus is with us! He empowers us to share his love and his truth with the world! We do not need to fear what others say or think. We have the answer to the problems of every human heart: reconciliation through Christ to a right relationship with God!

There are dozens of programs to teach us how to share the good news of Jesus Christ. (Most of you probably have heard of *"The Roman Road,"* among others) To lead others to Jesus, we must know His story, but more importantly, we must know *our* story with Him! Our relationship with Jesus and the impact it carries in our life will be the

> *"We have the answer to the problems of every human heart: reconciliation through Christ to a right relationship with God!"*

story that draws the world to our Jesus. And when I say *"the world,"* I don't necessarily mean Ethiopia or Taiwan or some faraway land of peoples. I mean Jackie from the grocery store, Ashley the dental hygienist, Scott the mechanic, your neighbor Jerry, and your cousin Pam! It's your world! When we carry a revelation of how much Jesus loves us, that will spill over into every aspect of our lives. Every interaction we have with others will have a flavor of that love and will carry one purpose: to let others be drawn to Jesus through us. How is that? By our demonstration of love to each person we encounter. We must change the filter with which we see the world from self-consciousness to Jesus-mindedness.

There's a story I love in John 21. It was after Jesus' resurrection, and seven of the disciples were together. It had to be a time of unsettledness for them, for Jesus told them to wait until they received power from the Holy Ghost, but that had yet to happen. So, Simon Peter did what he knew to do and told the others, *"I'm going fishing."* When we are not confident of our next move, how often do we revert to our old ways? The guys agreed and chimed in, *"We'll go with you!"* So, they went out and fished through the night and caught nothing. That result was a *"been there, done that"* moment for sure.

Let's read what happens next from John 21 (TPT): *"At dawn Jesus was standing on the shore but they didn't realize that it was him! He called out to them saying, 'Hey guys, did you catch any fish?' 'Not a thing,' they replied. Jesus shouted to them, 'Throw your net over the starboard side and you'll catch some!' And so they did as he said and they caught so many fish they couldn't even pull in the net!'"*

At that point, one of the disciples understood and declared, *"It's the Lord!"* Then Simon Peter leaped out of the boat and swam to shore! The others brought the boat ashore and saw a campfire with bread and fish. Jesus told them to bring some of their fish to cook as well. By now, they all knew who He was, and they shared breakfast. There is something about having a meal with someone that breaks down barriers and allows for easy communication (And for this ol' Florida girl, a breakfast cookout on the beach is about as good as it gets!) He took *time* with them to meet their needs. After all, they had been fishing all night. Jesus first enjoyed food and friendship with them before anything else.

Then Jesus began to question Peter, who had

denied Jesus before the crucifixion and no doubt carried some guilt and shame for those actions. Three times Peter denied Him, and three times Jesus asked Peter, *"Do you love Me?"* Peter answered that he did indeed love the Lord and Jesus restored their relationship. And three times, Jesus told him to *"feed My sheep."*

So what does this have to do with the Great Commission? I believe Jesus is first concerned about His relationship with us. Peter had been a staunch follower of Christ and had *"messed up"* and denied Him when things got hot. But he was not chastised nor condemned by Jesus instead he was given a chance to make things right. *And* after a great breakfast on the beach! For Peter, as a fisherman, that had to be a familiar and comfortable place. The relationship was restored when Peter humbly declared that yes, indeed, he did love the Lord. It was not about the disconnection of denial but the restoration of the relationship. At that moment of reconnection, Jesus gives Simon Peter his commission. When we submit ourselves to Jesus and declare our love for Him, He communicates His mission for us. Feed My sheep.

All that we as believers are called to do is in that simple phrase. Feed My sheep. When one *"feeds the sheep,"* it implies providing life-giving and life-sustaining nourishment. As a shepherd caring for his animals, it may also entail giving shelter from storms or protection from prey that would harm the sheep. Or the shepherd may go after a lost sheep, relieve the animal from fear or soothe the lamb in pain. We can easily apply that to the people we encounter who need love and care.

Another way to consider this is simple as well. Just do what He tells you. Do it now. Do it to your best ability. And then be ready for the next thing He tells you to do. We are not required to go out and hold tent revivals. (Well, some of us are. Sorry, Mario Murillo!) We are not required to design programs or activate armies. Instead, we *are* instructed to love others and allow the Holy Spirit to direct us to what specific action is needed. And when we do that, we are obedient children loving our Jesus by loving His people. And we fulfill the Great Commission...one person at a time.

**Just Do the Next Thing!**

Chapter Ten

# THE NEXT THING (FINALLY!)

Well, this conversation is nearly done! Perhaps you've recognized yourself on a page or two, and if so, *congratulations*! You made it to the end without giving up or throwing the book down! I'm embarrassed to admit I've thrown a book or two across my bedroom when I got to parts that were difficult to read. (The book about menopause hit the wall and fell flat, quite literally.)

To acknowledge where we have faults or weaknesses is always positive. Otherwise, we bumble around and stumble forward without much hope of inward change or outward improvement. Without the light of revelation from God's Word, the world is a dreary place.

My purpose in writing this book was to bring awareness to my fellow believers about how we can very easily slip from comfort to complacency. Even more importantly, to remind us how to stay connected to Jesus. So many books will tell you what's wrong. And what's wrong with that is there is no avenue toward growth and change. Through each chapter, my goal was to present God's viewpoint through His Word. I hope I've done that well enough that you already have a clear idea of what is next for you.

We are living in such exciting times! It's becoming easier to differentiate darkness from light. I like to use the analogy of a stage spotlight to relate how we see the world right now and the timing of Jesus coming for His bride, the church—*us*!

When a spotlight is opened wide, the light is broad and illuminates the entire stage. You can easily see all the actors and if there are people in the wings you can catch a glimpse of them as well. As that spotlight tightens, the light becomes more and more definitive till, at last, it is a small circle of light. The actor may step into the light, but one step back, and he's totally in darkness. Stage-wide, the grey areas are gone. Actors are either in the light, visible, or out of the light, invisible.

Additionally, as you hold a light (such as a flashlight) closer to an object, the light becomes more defined. We can relate that to time as we approach the season for Jesus' return. That spotlight beam is getting smaller as we move closer to His return. Those who walk in the light of God's Word, His redemptive plan, and His grace, are easily identified in the light. It's becoming easy to determine who is in the light

*"I believe that God is revealing to us who is walking and living in His light and who is not. Christians who may have been a bit shadowy in the wings need to step into the light."*

and who is not. I believe that God is revealing to us who is walking and living in His light and who is not. Christians who may have been a bit shadowy in the wings need to step into the light. No more hazy faith!

## RECOMMENDATIONS FOR REFLECTION
*(And hopefully, action!)*

1. **Recognize** error, sin, or separation from God.
2. **Repent.** Speak out loud what your heart confesses. God already knows, but it will do *you* good.
3. **Reconcile.** Ask for and receive forgiveness.
4. **Rejoice** that grace still abounds and accept it.
5. **Rededicate.** Recommit your life to the Lord. Do it publicly! Just tell somebody. *"Therefore whoever confesses Me before men, him I will also confess before My Father who is heaven"* *(Matthew 10:32).* The time for pride regarding what others think

is gone—no more facades—no more playing a role. Be authentic.

6. **Reconnect** with Jesus as your savior, your Lord, and your friend.

7. **Reestablish a relationship** with Him through praise, worship, prayer, and the baptism of the Holy Spirit.

8. **Rekindle your spirit.** Get fired up! It is a new day and a new way!

9. **Renew your mind.** You have the mind of Christ. (Hint: Use it!)

10. **Release** all doubt and fear to experience the power of God totally. Toss out old filters that once held you back: opinion of others, financial cost or benefit, social acceptance, indecision, the unknown, fear of rejection, *"what if."* Your only filter should be the Word and character of God. WWJD (What Would Jesus Do?) is not only catchy, but it is also correct and valuable and an excellent standard.

11. **Respond to the Holy Spirit** whenever He prompts or guides you. Don't be a slow learner!

12. **Restore broken relationships** with others. Unforgiveness from you or toward you is a hindrance. *"If it is possible, as much as depends on you, live peaceably with all men" (Romans 12:18).*

13. **Revisit** the *"old wells."* Recall those times of the anointing and presence of God in your life. Ask for the anointing to be poured out on you once again.

14. **Revel** in the grace God has given you as you live enthusiastically in righteousness, peace, and joy, true kingdom living!

15. **Resolve** to do kingdom business. Lead others to Jesus so they too can live a life of righteousness, peace, and joy. Do what Jesus did: preaching, teaching, and healing. *"Most assuredly, I say to you, he who believes in Me, the works that I do he will do also; And greater works than these he will do, because I go to my Father"* (John 14:12).

**Take Him at His Word.**

## Step In! Step Up! Step Out!

And let this always be said of you. From 1 Thessalonians 1:1b—3 (TPT):

*"May God's delightful grace and peace rest upon you. We are grateful to God for your lives and we always pray for you. For we remember before our God and Father how you put your faith into practice, how your love motivates you to serve others, and how unrelenting is your hope-filled patience in our Lord Jesus Christ".*"

# ABOUT THE AUTHOR

Pat Spell Blackwell is called and committed to connect people to Jesus and to a life of righteousness, peace, and joy. Educated, trained, experienced, and ordained, she practices her faith every day, is motivated by love, and lives in hope. She has endured struggles enough to have authentic faith and has experienced victories enough to daily celebrate the goodness of God.

An ordained minister since 2000, Pat earned master's degrees in Guidance and Counseling and in Theology and received her doctorate in Christian Counseling. She has served her church and her community in a variety of ministry settings including home groups, single moms, crisis pregnancy center, deaf ministry, and youth, as well as hospital chaplain and private practice Christian counseling.

She and her husband Elwood reared six daughters and have seven granddaughters. Following Elwood's death in 2020, Pat moved from her hometown in Central Florida to Spokane Washington, where she is writing and availing herself to whatever God has for this new season and is attempting to un-spoil a very precocious six-pound poodle name Ziva David.

# RECOMMENDED READING

To Encourage Your Kingdom Living

*Kept for the Master's Use* by Francis Ridley Havergol

*The Master is Calling* by Lynne Hammond

*Life Together* by Dietrich Bonhoeffer

*The Cost of Discipleship* by Dietrich Bonhoeffer

*Courageous Leadership* by Bill Hybels

*The Final Quest* by Rick Joiner

*Vessels of Fire and Glory* by Mario Murillo

*Prayers That Avail Much* by Germaine Copeland

*7 Essential to Gain Influence for Success in Life, Ministry, & Business* by Charlana Kelly

*If Not for the Grace of God* by Joyce Meyer

***The Biggest Lie in the History of Christianity*** by Matthew Kelly

***The Walk of the Spirit, the Walk of Power*** by Dave Roberson

***Disappointment with God*** by Philip Yancy

***Good Morning, Holy Spirit*** by Benny Hinn

***Activating the Prophetic*** by Clay Nash

***The Knowledge of the Holy*** by A.W. Tozer

***Crazy Love*** by Francis Chan

***Rediscovering the Kingdom*** by Miles Monroe

***The Key to Triumphant Living*** by Jack Taylor

***Me and My Big Mouth*** by Joyce Meyer

***The Kirk and the Covenant: The Stalwart Courage of John Knox*** by Douglas Wilson

***Critical Mass*** by Mario Murillo

***Edgewise*** by Marion Murillo

***The True Nature of God*** by Andrew Wommack

CPSIA information can be obtained
at www.ICGtesting.com
Printed in the USA
BVHW070856120122
625988BV00005B/369